Crystel Lynn Smith and Dr. Sherri M. Yoder

Today I Will Serve. Copyright© 2018 by Crystel Lynn Smith and Dr. Sherri M. Yoder.

All rights reserved. Printed in the United States of America. No part of this book may be used or reproduced in any manner whatsoever without written permission of the authors.

For information:

Optimum Impact, LLC, P.O. Box 1991, Front Royal, VA 22630

Cover Artwork Courtesy of Callan Costa Smith

ISBN-13: 978-1717017123
ISBN-10: 1717017126

First Edition

Join the movement! #Grateful2Serve

Today I Will Serve

Crystel Lynn Smith & Dr. Sherri M. Yoder

Join the movement! #Grateful2Serve

Walk through a life-changing journey of serving! Commit with us for the next 60 days to transforming your life and the lives of others through a simple daily plan of intentional serving.

Today I Will Serve provides you with an action plan of serving others. Use the daily planner to intentionally write down how and whom you will serve. Gain inspiration and direction from the daily scriptures on the bottom of each page. Give and live an abundant blessed life of service to others!

God created each one of us beautifully and with unique talents and gifts. It is our obligation and privilege to share those talents and gifts with others.

By serving others we:

> Fulfill God's purpose in our lives.

"For I know the plans I have for you," declares the LORD, "plans to prosper you and not to harm you, plans to give you hope and a future."

– Jeremiah 29:11

> Bless others and receive blessings.

"The one who blesses others is abundantly blessed; those who help others are helped."

– Proverbs 11:25

Join the movement! #Grateful2Serve

Dear Reader,

We are humbled and honored to serve you!

Can you imagine what the world would be like if every day every person chose to seek out the needs of others and then just serve? There would never be a need that went unmet!

Living a life of intentional serving, sharing of our talents and gifts, has been life changing for us, and often, life changing for those we serve. We want to share this blessed life with you, to serve you.

Serving can be so simple to do yet we often get overwhelmed with thoughts like, *"I don't have money to give,"* or *"I just don't have the time."* Or *"I'm a mess. How could I serve or help anyone else?"*

Serving others can be done in the simplest form. We often serve without even realizing it. A kind word, a "thinking about you" text or phone call, a little bit of advice, and an invitation to get together, are all acts of service.

Sometimes it takes someone to share that they feel like a mess to connect with others who are feeling the same. Remember, God works in mysterious ways! Someone else may be feeling exactly like you and need to hear your story.

Serving others provides immediate rewards. We instantly focus on the needs of others rather than our own challenges, giving us a sense of purpose and meaning that we are all seeking.

We created Today I Will Serve to provide you with the opportunity to see how you can serve, and then by writing the opportunities down put your service into action. As you intentionally serve, you will discover or rediscover a life of meaning and purpose and be abundantly blessed!

Whom will you serve today? Your God? Your family? Your friends? Your neighbor? A stranger? All of the above? There are limitless opportunities for service. Intentionally decide whom and how you will serve each day, write it down, and then serve!

Join us in serving, blessing, and being more blessed than you ever imagined possible! Let's create a movement of service to others! We would love to hear how you serve or how you've been blessed by someone's service to you.

Join the movement! #Grateful2Serve

Share your stories of service with us via email at:

Crystel@CrystelandSherri.com
or
Sherri@CrystelandSherri.com
or
#Grateful2Serve to join the movement!

With unconditional gratitude and service,

Sherri and Crystel

Today ___/___/20__ I Will Serve

My God

_____

_____

My Family

_____

_____

My Friends

_____

_____

My Neighbors

_____

_____

A Stranger

_____

_____

"God is not unjust; he will not forget your work and the love you have shown him as you have helped his people and continue to help them."

Hebrews 6:10

Join the movement! #Grateful2Serve

♦

Deliberative, diligent, and dutiful acts of service are indeed work; Work that when done, produces joy, gratitude, and purpose!

♦

Today ___/___/20__ I Will Serve

My God

_____

_____

My Family

_____

_____

My Friends

_____

_____

My Neighbors

_____

_____

A Stranger

_____

_____

"You, my brothers and sisters, were called to be free. But do not use your freedom to indulge the flesh; rather, serve one another humbly in love."

Galatians 5:13

Join the movement! #Grateful2Serve

♦

Service is selfless. It is the opposite of life's most debilitating habit: selfishness. You were created to serve others. Today, allow your own desires to fall away and chose how you will free yourself from selfishness and serve!

♦

Today ___/___/20__ I Will Serve

My God

_____

_____

My Family

_____

_____

My Friends

_____

_____

My Neighbors

_____

_____

A Stranger

_____

_____

"Therefore, I urge you, brothers and sisters, in view of God's mercy, to offer your bodies as a living sacrifice, holy and pleasing to God—this is your true and proper worship."

Romans 12:1

Join the movement! #Grateful2Serve

♦

If God has given you hands, use them to serve, not to pursue evil. If God has given you a tongue, speak life to others, not death. God has given you a desire to serve Him and others. Make that desire manifest today.

♦

Today ___/___/20__ I Will Serve

My God

_____

_____

My Family

_____

_____

My Friends

_____

_____

My Neighbors

_____

_____

A Stranger

_____

_____

"But be sure to fear the LORD and serve him faithfully with all your heart; consider what great things He has done for you."

1 Samuel 12:24

Join the movement! #Grateful2Serve

◆

Take a moment today to thank the Lord for His generous gifts to you. Write down every way you've been blessed and how you could serve whether it be with your time, your words, or even your finances. Then, ask Him how you can honor Him by using those gifts to serve others.

◆

Today ___/___/20__ I Will Serve

My God

_____

_____

My Family

_____

_____

My Friends

_____

_____

My Neighbors

_____

_____

A Stranger

_____

_____

"Whoever serves me must follow me; and where I am, my servant also will be. My Father will honor the one who serves me."

John 12:26

Join the movement! #Grateful2Serve

Jesus served everyone, even those who society says should be discarded or despised. We are called to follow Jesus' lead. How can you make today a day of sacrificial service, particularly to someone you believe is least deserving?

Join the movement! #Grateful2Serve

Today, ___/___/20__, I will serve

My God

_____

_____

My Family

_____

_____

My Friends

_____

_____

My Neighbors

_____

_____

A Stranger

_____

_____

"Never be lacking in zeal, but keep your spiritual fervor, serving the Lord."

Romans 12:11

Join the movement! #Grateful2Serve

♦

We can easily become exhausted (mentally and physically) when serving others, without a heart or serving. May you be reminded today that your ultimate act of service is to God. He will sustain you when you truly seek to Honor Him with the work of your hands and mind. And if your intent is to serve without gaining anything in return, merely the act of service will provide a sense of accomplishment and reward!

♦

Today ___/___/20__ I Will Serve

My God

_____

_____

My Family

_____

_____

My Friends

_____

_____

My Neighbors

_____

_____

A Stranger

_____

_____

"For even the Son of Man did not come to be served, but to serve, and to give his life as a ransom for many."

Mark 10:45

Join the movement! #Grateful2Serve

♦

When your feet hit the floor this morning, ask yourself these two questions: "Whom will I serve today? How will I keep my mind's eye on serving others, forsaking my own needs?" Our world and sometimes our minds say we should first think about ourselves. And God commands us to put others first. By putting others' needs first, we immediately take the focus off our own challenges and struggles, freeing us from worry, resentment, and guilt that we often feel when we are focused on ourselves.

♦

Today ___/___/20__ I Will Serve

My God

_____

_____

My Family

_____

_____

My Friends

_____

_____

My Neighbors

_____

_____

A Stranger

_____

_____

"Each of you should use whatever gift you have received to serve others, as faithful stewards of God's grace in its various forms."

1 Peter 4:10

Join the movement! #Grateful2Serve

♦

Self-help books say it's all about "YOU!" Well, they're right! It is all about you...the gifts with which you've been endowed. Now...go give them! Share your gifts with others today, on purpose, and watch your world explode with purpose and passion!

♦

Today ___/___/20__ I Will Serve

My God

_____

_____

My Family

_____

_____

My Friends

_____

_____

My Neighbors

_____

_____

A Stranger

_____

_____

"But be very careful to keep the commandment and the law that Moses the servant of the LORD gave you: to love the LORD your God, to walk in obedience to him, to keep his commands, to hold fast to him and to serve him with all your heart and with all your soul."

Joshua 22:5

Join the movement! #Grateful2Serve

♦

Bills, errands, work demands, family pressures…they all amount to that dreaded six-letter word, "STRESS!" Only, however, if we allow it. If your only goal today is to serve the Lord your God and others, with all your heart and soul, there is no room for stress, as your mind and heart will be filled with the joy that comes from serving.

♦

Join the movement! #Grateful2Serve

Today ___/____20__ *I will serve*

My God

_____

_____

My Family

_____

_____

My Friends

_____

_____

My Neighbors

_____

_____

A Stranger

_____

_____

"Give, and it will be given to you. A good measure, pressed down, shaken together and running over, will be poured into your lap. For with the measure you use, it will be measured to you."

Luke 6:38

Join the movement! #Grateful2Serve

♦

Ah, giving. This can prove particularly hard during the holiday season when everyone seems to have a hand out for help. Today, you are challenged to give, unabashedly give. Give, and know that a return greater than you can imagine will be your reward, when you give and expect nothing in return.

♦

Today ___/___/20___ I Will Serve

My God

_____

_____

My Family

_____

_____

My Friends

_____

_____

My Neighbors

_____

_____

A Stranger

_____

_____

"Share with the Lord's people who are in need. Practice hospitality."

Romans 12:13

Join the movement! #Grateful2Serve

◆

You know that homeless guy standing wearily on the median next to the stoplight of your shopping center? He's asking for help. What will you do? Will you be jaded? Will you look away? Or will you reach into your shopping bag for a bottle of water to quench his thirst? Remember, we never know when we are entertaining angels. Serve without judgment today!

◆

Today ___/___/20__ I Will Serve

My God

_____

_____

My Family

_____

_____

My Friends

_____

_____

My Neighbors

_____

_____

A Stranger

_____

_____

"Be devoted to one another in love. Honor one another above yourselves."

Romans 12:10

Join the movement! #Grateful2Serve

◆

This is a toughie! Have you ever thought, "Sure, I'll devote myself to ____, when they devote themselves to me!?" This is an opportunity for you! God calls us to count others ABOVE ourselves. That means we can't make our service conditional! Be unconditional and unreasonable in your service today!

◆

Join the movement! #Grateful2Serve

Today ___/___/20__ I Will Serve

My God

_____

_____

My Family

_____

_____

My Friends

_____

_____

My Neighbors

_____

_____

A Stranger

_____

_____

"*How much more, then, will the blood of Christ, who through the eternal Spirit offered himself unblemished to God, cleanse our consciences from acts that lead to death, so that we may serve the living God!*"

Hebrews 9:14

Join the movement! #Grateful2Serve

♦

We have been granted the greatest gift of all time…ultimate pardon of our sin, of our wrong-doing. If you received the greatest gift you could imagine, would you hoard it? Or would you share it with others? Forgiveness, once you've received it, is a gift you cannot wait to share! Who will you serve today by offering them forgiveness?

♦

Join the movement! #Grateful2Serve

Today ___/___/20___ *I Will Serve*

My God

_____

_____

My Family

_____

_____

My Friends

_____

_____

My Neighbors

_____

_____

A Stranger

_____

_____

"And you, my son Solomon, acknowledge the God of your father, and serve him with wholehearted devotion and with a willing mind, for the LORD searches every heart and understands every desire and every thought. If you seek him, he will be found by you; but if you forsake him, he will reject you forever."

1 Chronicles 28:9

Join the movement! #Grateful2Serve

◆

Today, search your heart. Ask God to reveal your hidden desires to serve others. Ask Him to forgive you where you've fallen short. Ask Him to give you wisdom to set things right. Ask Him for a pure heart and clean hands. He is patiently waiting! You may have a friend who's patiently waiting for an apology and to mend your friendship. Will you serve them today?

◆

Today ___/___/20__ *I Will Serve*

My God

_____

_____

My Family

_____

_____

My Friends

_____

_____

My Neighbors

_____

_____

A Stranger

_____

_____

"The greatest among you will be your servant."

Matthew 23:11

Join the movement! #Grateful2Serve

♦

Are you a manager, business owner, or boss? Are you a parent or caregiver? You have an incredible charge: To serve those who would be considered your followers. If you truly desire to lead, you will pick up the broom handle with gladness, and serve. May your hands get dirty in service to others today!

♦

Join the movement! #Grateful2Serve

Today ___/___/20___ I Will Serve

My God

_____

_____

My Family

_____

_____

My Friends

_____

_____

My Neighbors

_____

_____

A Stranger

_____

_____

"If you love those who love you, what reward will you get? Are not even the tax collectors doing that?"

Matthew 5:46

Join the movement! #Grateful2Serve

◆

And now, it gets real! Picture that person you are irritated by, or the one you despise. Now, read Matthew 5:46 again. It's so easy to serve someone who loves us in return. How about those who accuse us? Those who despise us? Look for your opportunity to be blessed today by serving someone you may consider to be undeserving of your love.

◆

Today ___/___/20__ I Will Serve

My God

_____

_____

My Family

_____

_____

My Friends

_____

_____

My Neighbors

_____

_____

A Stranger

_____

_____

"Whoever brings blessing will be enriched, and one who waters will himself be watered."

Proverbs 11:25

Join the movement! #Grateful2Serve

♦

There are far too many of us wishing for good to befall us. What if we worked at it? What if we delivered value to others by serving them? What would happen today if you devoted all your efforts to planting and watering relationship seeds? We bet you wouldn't be sitting around waiting for the good. No, you'd be delivering enrichment to others and would no doubt receive it in return. Schedule some time today to meet with someone and spend the entire time together focused on them, their needs, and how you can serve them.

♦

Today ___/___/20__ I Will Serve

My God

_____

_____

My Family

_____

_____

My Friends

_____

_____

My Neighbors

_____

_____

A Stranger

_____

_____

"So then, as we have opportunity, let us do good to everyone, and especially to those who are of the household of faith."

Galatians 6:10

Join the movement! #Grateful2Serve

♦

You have a choice of whom you serve. God calls us to serve everyone. When we determine who is, or is not, worthy, we defy God's Word. May your day be filled with gladness as you serve everyone, even those who do not see the world as you do. Who will you serve? The grocery clerk? The person behind you at the drive-thru? Your child's teacher? Someone with a different faith? Your competitor?

♦

Today ___/___/20__ *I Will Serve*

My God

_____

_____

My Family

_____

_____

My Friends

_____

_____

My Neighbors

_____

_____

A Stranger

_____

_____

"But love your enemies, and do good, and lend, expecting nothing in return, and your reward will be great, and you will be sons of the Most High, for he is kind to the ungrateful and the evil."

Luke 6:35

Join the movement! #Grateful2Serve

♦

Do you ever wonder why "bad" people seem to prosper? Consider this. Your righteousness is as filthy rags (Isaiah 64:6). We are ALL sinners in God's eyes. Yes, even us. Even you. Yet, thanks be to Jesus, those who trust in Him have been redeemed! If that's true, then you are no more deserving of blessings than the next person. So, what are you waiting for? Go and bless your neighbor (worthy or not in your eyes) today!

♦

Today ___/___/20__ I Will Serve

My God

_____

_____

My Family

_____

_____

My Friends

_____

_____

My Neighbors

_____

_____

A Stranger

_____

_____

"I have shown you in every way, by laboring like this, that you must support the weak. And remember the words of the Lord Jesus, that He said, 'It is more blessed to give than to receive."

Acts 20:35

Join the movement! #Grateful2Serve

♦

Think about your community, your work, your home, your church. Now, picture one who is "weak." Will you judge or serve them? Today is your opportunity to serve someone who is weaker than you. They don't need judgment. They desperately need your service as you act as the hands of Christ.

♦

Today ___/___/20__ I Will Serve

My God

_____

_____

My Family

_____

_____

My Friends

_____

_____

My Neighbors

_____

_____

A Stranger

_____

_____

"For we are his workmanship, created in Christ Jesus for good works, which God prepared beforehand, that we should walk in them."

Ephesians 2:10

Join the movement! #Grateful2Serve

♦

DaVinci? He's got nothing on God! No matter what the mirror told you this morning, YOU are God's masterpiece. He is painting an unrivaled canvas in the person of you. And the world needs that masterpiece. It needs YOU! So, what are you waiting for? Get our there and give of yourself today!

♦

Join the movement! #Grateful2Serve

Today ___/___/20__ *I Will Serve*

My God

_____

_____

My Family

_____

_____

My Friends

_____

_____

My Neighbors

_____

_____

A Stranger

_____

_____

"All Scripture is God-breathed and is useful for teaching, rebuking, correcting and training in righteousness, so that the servant of God may be thoroughly equipped for every good work."

2 Timothy 3:16-17

Join the movement! #Grateful2Serve

♦

God's Word is sufficient for all your needs. It answers all your questions. Use it to test what we say here. Use it to draw close to Him. Use His Word to accomplish the purpose He has set forth, uniquely for you!

♦

Today ___ / ___ / 20__ *I Will Serve*

My God

_____

_____

My Family

_____

_____

My Friends

_____

_____

My Neighbors

_____

_____

A Stranger

_____

_____

"As it is written: "They have freely scattered their gifts to the poor; their righteousness endures forever."

2 Corinthians 9:9

Join the movement! #Grateful2Serve

♦

How "free" are you with the gifts with which you've been granted? It's easy to think that material possessions (house, car, etc.... you know, those things we've come to believe are essential) are indicators of success. When you realize that every gift you have has been granted to you by God Almighty, you are freed to stop clinging so tightly to them. You can give them away, either to God or to others. You can truly be "free" from what society says should matter.

♦

Today ___/___/20__ I Will Serve

My God

_____

_____

My Family

_____

_____

My Friends

_____

_____

My Neighbors

_____

_____

A Stranger

_____

_____

"Work willingly at whatever you do, as though you were working for the Lord rather than for people. Remember that the Lord will give you an inheritance as your reward, and that the Master you are serving is Christ."

Colossians 3:23-24

Join the movement! #Grateful2Serve

♦

It's time to stop thinking about you. It's high time you focus on the fact that you are living and breathing because you have a job to do: to serve others. That's what your God created you for. Your ultimate service is to Him. Will you tell Him, "Not today God, Today is all about me?," or will you say, "Yes, I am willing to serve. Show me the way!"

♦

Today ___/___/20___ *I Will Serve*

My God

_____

_____

My Family

_____

_____

My Friends

_____

_____

My Neighbors

_____

_____

A Stranger

_____

_____

"And the King will say, 'I tell you the truth, when you did it to one of the least of these my brothers and sisters, you were doing it to me!'

Matthew 25:40

Join the movement! #Grateful2Serve

◆

Can you imagine? You see someone in need? Someone your community decides isn't worthwhile. You choose to serve them…because…you are doing it for the King! Whoa! What an opportunity! Go serve them and ultimately serve your King today!

◆

Today ___/___/20___ I Will Serve

My God

_____

_____

My Family

_____

_____

My Friends

_____

_____

My Neighbors

_____

_____

A Stranger

_____

_____

"Feed the hungry and help those in trouble. Then your light will shine out from the darkness, and the darkness around you will be as bright as noon."

Isaiah 58:10

Join the movement! #Grateful2Serve

♦

We are a society of doubt and skepticism. We see people visiting food banks and shelters and we piously think to ourselves, "Clearly they don't want to work." God calls us to HELP, not to evaluate whether someone is worthy of help. Remember, you (along with the rest of us) weren't worthy of forgiveness and God graciously granted it to us anyway! Find a food bank, shelter, or other cause to serve today!

♦

Today ___/___/20__ *I Will Serve*

My God

_____

_____

My Family

_____

_____

My Friends

_____

_____

My Neighbors

_____

_____

A Stranger

_____

_____

"Each of you should give what you have decided in your heart to give not reluctantly or under compulsion, for God loves a cheerful giver."

2 Corinthians 9:7

Join the movement! #Grateful2Serve

♦

As members of our communities, we are constantly asked for monetary contributions. Sometimes we give out of obligation and sometimes out of excitement for a cause we strongly believe in. Now, imagine that you are asked to give, and you do it out of the abundance of your heart! You say to yourself, "I choose to give because my heart won't let me not!" This, is giving as a cheerful giver. What organization or part of your community could you serve today?

♦

Today ___/___/20___ I Will Serve

My God

_____

_____

My Family

_____

_____

My Friends

_____

_____

My Neighbors

_____

_____

A stranger

_____

_____

"For the entire law is fulfilled in keeping this one command: Love your neighbor as yourself."

Galatians 5:14

Join the movement! #Grateful2Serve

♦

We recently watched an episode of "Fear Thy Neighbor" on the ID channel. The fact that there is a show entitled as such speaks to the lack of fellowship in the verse above. "Love your neighbor as yourself." Really? That's what I'm supposed to do? YES!!! If you have a grievance with your neighbor, today is your opportunity to settle it! They are worth as much as you!

♦

Join the movement! #Grateful2Serve

Today ___/___/20__ I Will Serve

My God

_____

_____

My Family

_____

_____

My Friends

_____

_____

My Neighbors

_____

_____

A Stranger

_____

_____

"This is a trustworthy saying. And I want you to stress these things, so that those who have trusted in God may be careful to devote themselves to doing what is good. These things are excellent and profitable for everyone."

Titus 3:8

Join the movement! #Grateful2Serve

♦

People say terrible things about us sometimes. Would you believe us if we said it's your choice to own that or not? Serve yourself today. Trust in the Lord that His gifts in you will be revealed. Do not fear what man will do to you.

♦

Today ___/___/20__ I Will Serve

My God

_____

_____

My Family

_____

_____

My Friends

_____

_____

My Neighbors

_____

_____

A Stranger

_____

_____

"Make sure that nobody pays back wrong for wrong, but always strive to do what is good for each other and for everyone else."

1 Thessalonians 5:15

Join the movement! #Grateful2Serve

♦

Serve everyone as is you were serving a child, freely, lovingly, abundantly, and excitedly! When we feed our children, we do not expect anything in return. Then, why when we feed our neighbors, do we expect to be invited to their home for dinner?

♦

Join the movement! #Grateful2Serve

Today ___/___/20__ I Will Serve

My God

_____

_____

My Family

_____

_____

My Friends

_____

_____

My Neighbors

_____

_____

A Stranger

_____

_____

"Little children, let us not love with word or with tongue, but in deed and truth."

1 John 3:18

Join the movement! #Grateful2Serve

♦

So often we say we are going to serve with the best of intentions. Yet, we often find reasons that we can't fulfill our promises. Today we challenge you to first be honest about your ability to serve. Second, commit to serving. Finally, act immediately. You might say, "I'll pray for you right now;" or "I'll call that person for you right now." Speak and serve your truth today!

♦

Today ___/___/20__ I Will Serve

My God

_____

_____

My Family

_____

_____

My Friends

_____

_____

My Neighbors

_____

_____

A Stranger

_____

_____

"Then I heard the voice of the Lord, saying, 'Whom shall I send, and who will go for Us?' Then I said, 'Here am I. Send me!'"

Isaiah 6:8

Join the movement! #Grateful2Serve

♦

Will you be a servant of the Lord? Will you say, "Hey, God, here I am! I'm going to do what you want!" If this is you, ask God to direct your next steps. He will deliver and reward you in ways that no one can expect!

♦

Today ___/___/20__ I Will Serve

My God

_____

_____

My Family

_____

_____

My Friends

_____

_____

My Neighbors

_____

_____

A Stranger

_____

_____

"Now that I, your Lord and Teacher, have washed your feet, you also should wash one another's feet. I have set you an example that you should do as I have done for you."

John 13:14-15

Join the movement! #Grateful2Serve

♦

We are called to serve in such a way that we count others as better than ourselves. Would you wash your neighbors feet? Perhaps not literally. You do, however, have daily opportunities to serve by doing things that you would rather not. How will you wash feet today?

♦

Today ___/___/20__ I Will Serve

My God

_____

_____

My Family

_____

_____

My Friends

_____

_____

My Neighbors

_____

_____

A Stranger

_____

_____

"And he sat down and called the twelve. And he said to them, "If anyone would be first, he must be last of all and servant of all."

Mark 9:35

Join the movement! #Grateful2Serve

♦

Who doesn't want a seat at the table? Your seat at the table comes when your first give yours up to someone else. That's what a true servant does, makes room for another. Who will you give your seat to today?

♦

Join the movement! #Grateful2Serve

Today ___/___/20___ *I Will Serve*

My God

_____

_____

My Family

_____

_____

My Friends

_____

_____

My Neighbors

_____

_____

A Stranger

_____

_____

"Whoever is generous to the poor lends to the Lord, and he will repay him for his deed."

Proverbs 19:17

Join the movement! #Grateful2Serve

♦

Do you give money to those who can benefit you? Or do you lend to those who cannot repay you? Choose generosity today, regardless of the benefactor, and you will experience the Lord's blessing! Give and it shall be given unto you!

♦

Today ___/___/20__ *I Will Serve*

My God

_____

_____

My Family

_____

_____

My Friends

_____

_____

My Neighbors

_____

_____

A Stranger

_____

_____

"But if anyone has the world's goods and sees his brother in need, yet closes his heart against him, how does God's love abide in him?"

1 John 3:17

Join the movement! #Grateful2Serve

♦

It's easy to look away from the afflicted. It's easy to judge those who are asking for help. But what if our judge isn't ourselves? What if our judge is God? Will that change how we serve? What if God were walking right beside you every moment of every day? Because He is. Who will you serve as if God was there to witness your acts of service firsthand?

♦

Today ___/___/20__ I Will Serve

My God

_____

_____

My Family

_____

_____

My Friends

_____

_____

My Neighbors

_____

_____

A Stranger

_____

_____

"Whoever oppresses a poor man insults his Maker, but he who is generous to the needy honors him."

Proverbs 14:31

Join the movement! #Grateful2Serve

♦

Do you have the ability to give, but decide to sell instead? Think about your opportunity to serve today. Sometimes we need to make money; Other times we have the power to bless someone. Chose someone or something to offer your product or service for free today.

♦

Today ___/___/20__ I Will Serve

My God

_____

_____

My Family

_____

_____

My Friends

_____

_____

My Neighbors

_____

_____

A Stranger

_____

_____

"You shall give to him freely, and your heart shall not be grudging when you give to him, because for this the Lord your God will bless you in all your work and in all that you undertake."

Deuteronomy 15:10

Join the movement! #Grateful2Serve

♦

What if you were to forgive a debt? Many would say you are weak. The reality is you are a servant. It's not about being taken advantage of, it's about sharing in abundance with good faith. Consider your opportunity to relieve someone's debt or even forgive a debt owed to you today!

♦

Today ___/___/20__ I Will Serve

My God

_____

_____

My Family

_____

_____

My Friends

_____

_____

My Neighbors

_____

_____

A Stranger

_____

_____

"For there will never cease to be poor in the land. Therefore, I command you, 'You shall open wide your hand to your brother, to the needy and to the poor, in your land."

Deuteronomy 15:11

Join the movement! #Grateful2Serve

◆

Take stock of your blessings. Is there something you can do without? Now is your opportunity to be a blessing to someone. Do you have a bounty of gifts? Do you have clothes you no longer wear, furniture collecting dust, books sitting in boxes? Today is your opportunity to share them with others!

◆

Today ___/___/20__ I Will Serve

My God

_____

_____

My Family

_____

_____

My Friends

_____

_____

My Neighbors

_____

_____

A Stranger

_____

_____

"Whoever has a bountiful eye will be blessed, for he shares his bread with the poor."

Proverbs 22:9

Join the movement! #Grateful2Serve

♦

If you looked in your cupboard right now, we bet you'd see many unused cans/boxes of food. What would give you cause to share them? If there was a food shortage, would you harbor them? Or would you share your food stores? What if the neighbor simply needed a bag of noodles? Would you give it to them? Today, is your opportunity to serve! Find a person or a family who needs to be fed and share the food that's been in your cupboard for more than 30 days.

♦

Join the movement! #Grateful2Serve

Today ___/___/20___ I Will Serve

My God

_____

_____

My Family

_____

_____

My Friends

_____

_____

My Neighbors

_____

_____

A Stranger

_____

_____

"For I was hungry, and you gave me food. I was thirsty, and you gave me drink. I was a stranger and you welcomed me. I was naked, and you clothed me."

Matthew 25:35-36

Join the movement! #Grateful2Serve

♦

Ask yourself today: "Do I have the capacity to love a stranger? Do I have the ability to give them food and shelter?" Remember, you may be entertaining angels. Give of what you have been given. A simple hug, a kind word, a note, a phone call, a text, a song, a sandwich, or a warm bed can be life changing for who you serve, and for you!

♦

Join the movement! #Grateful2Serve

Today ___/___/20__ I Will Serve

My God

_____

_____

My Family

_____

_____

My Friends

_____

_____

My Neighbors

_____

_____

A Stranger

_____

_____

"Do nothing out of selfish ambition or vain conceit. Rather, in humility value others above yourselves, not looking to your own interests but each of you to the interests of the others."

Philippians 2:3-4

Join the movement! #Grateful2Serve

◆

Being a spouse can be particularly challenging…when called to give. The resentment that sets in because of the other's lack to do something for us…it's unbearable at times. This is a direct result of our lack of ability to look to how we can serve them, while focusing on ourselves, our own wants, desires, and needs. Focus on serving your loved ones, rather than your own wants and needs and that resentment will diminish! And if you and your loved one focus solely on how you can serve each other, both of you will have every need, desire, and want met! Today, abandon selfish reason for serving and embrace service for the sake of service.

◆

Today ___/___/20___ *I Will Serve*

My God

_____

_____

My Family

_____

_____

My Friends

_____

_____

My Neighbors

_____

_____

A Stranger

_____

_____

"In the same way, let your light shine before others, so that they may see your good works and give glory to your Father who is in heaven."

Matthew 5:17

Join the movement! #Grateful2Serve

♦

Selflessness will never be accomplished in secret. When you truly want to serve, you accept that others may not know that you were the one serving. You welcome anonymity. You will be rewarded for your good deeds. In due time. You serve because that's what you're called to do. Today chose someone to serve in secret. A note on their car, a bag of groceries at their door, or a gift in their mailbox. Intentionally, and secretly, serve today.

♦

Today ___/___/20__ *I Will Serve*

My God

_____

_____

My Family

_____

_____

My Friends

_____

_____

My Neighbors

_____

_____

A Stranger

_____

_____

"And let us not grow weary of doing good, for in due season we will reap, if we do not give up."

Galatians 6:9

Join the movement! #Grateful2Serve

♦

Forget the nay-sayers. They say everyone is out for something. They say you're a "sucker" for doing what you do. God's Word says you will be rewarded for your service. God says you will reap the good of what you sow. So, give, serve, and be blessed!

♦

Join the movement! #Grateful2Serve

Today ____/____/20__ I Will Serve

My God

_____

_____

My Family

_____

_____

My Friends

_____

_____

My Neighbors

_____

_____

A Stranger

_____

_____

"Bear one another's burdens, and so fulfill the law of Christ."

Galatians 6:2

Join the movement! #Grateful2Serve

♦

Whose burdens are you bearing today? Is your loved one hurting? Are you hurting with them? Does your heart weep alongside them? If not, ask God to give you a desire to bear your brother's/sister's burden. He will answer your prayer.

♦

Today ___/___/20___ I Will Serve

My God

_____

_____

My Family

_____

_____

My Friends

_____

_____

My Neighbors

_____

_____

A Stranger

_____

_____

"We who are strong have an obligation to bear with the failings of the weak, and not to please ourselves."

Romans 15:11

Join the movement! #Grateful2Serve

♦

Think about those who have succumbed to alcohol or drug addiction. They have become weak in the faith...not weak in the worthiness of their love of God. Serve them with love and patience and endurance. They need you.

♦

Today ___/___/20__ I Will Serve

My God

_____

_____

My Family

_____

_____

My Friends

_____

_____

My Neighbors

_____

_____

A Stranger

_____

_____

"Whoever despises his neighbor is a sinner but blessed is he who is generous to the poor."

Proverbs 14:21

Join the movement! #Grateful2Serve

◆

Look at your neighbor. Are they like you? Are they different from you? Of course, they are different. If you and your neighbor were exactly the same, one of you would be unnecessary. Have you taken time to know them and find out how you are different and how you can serve them? Imagine if every person served one neighbor every day. The world would be full of abundance, grace, and purpose! What neighbor, either literal, (in your neighborhood) or figurative, (in your workplace, church, board, club or organization) will you serve today?

◆

Today ____/____/20____ I Will Serve

My God

_____

_____

My Family

_____

_____

My Friends

_____

_____

My Neighbors

_____

_____

A Stranger

_____

_____

"And the crowds asked him, "What then shall we do?" And he answered them, "Whoever has two tunics is to share with him who has none, and whoever has food is to do likewise."

Luke 3:10-11

Join the movement! #Grateful2Serve

♦

When was the last time you told someone how wonderful you thought they were? Your spouse, your child, your coworker? We all need to feel loved and valued. Find someone today to lift and serve with your words.

♦

Today ___/___/20___ *I Will Serve*

My God

_____

_____

My Family

_____

_____

My Friends

_____

_____

My Neighbors

_____

_____

A Stranger

_____

_____

"Give to the one who begs from you, and do not refuse the one who would borrow from you."

Matthew 5:42

Join the movement! #Grateful2Serve

♦

The world if full of people known as "the needy". Are we all not needy? We all need grace, forgiveness, mercy, love, respect, friends, and family. The list goes on. How many times do we ignore those we identify as needy? Is it up to us to determine whether someone is genuine in their request for help? Is it up to us to say they're worth our time? Our resources? Our effort? If someone is "needy," we can fulfill their need. Because we, you, all of us, will eventually, in some way, shape or form, be needy too. We challenge you to fulfill a need of someone who the world sees as needy today.

♦

Today ___/___/20__ I Will Serve

My God

_____

_____

My Family

_____

_____

My Friends

_____

_____

My Neighbors

_____

_____

A Stranger

_____

_____

"Sell your possessions and give to the needy. Provide yourselves with moneybags that do not grow old, with a treasure in the heavens that does not fail, where no thief approaches and no moth destroys. For where your treasure is, there will your heart be also."

Luke 12:33-34

Join the movement! #Grateful2Serve

♦

If you looked at your "stuff" today, what could you identify as necessary? Less than 20% of what you have? We need food, drink, shelter, love and faith. Yet we collect material things in abundance. Do you need a guest bedroom? Or could you serve a family with your extra bed or dresser. Do you need three sets of dishes or could you bless a family with one? Do you need a pantry full of food? Or could you feed a struggling family? Take inventory today and turn your excess into blessings!

♦

Join the movement! #Grateful2Serve

Today ____/____/20___ I Will Serve

My God

_____

_____

My Family

_____

_____

My Friends

_____

_____

My Neighbors

_____

_____

A Stranger

_____

_____

"For who is the greater, one who reclines at table or one who serves? Is it not the one who reclines at table? But I am among you as the one who serves."

Luke 22:27

Join the movement! #Grateful2Serve

♦

Leadership traditionally has been thought of as a prestigious position of authority. However, you can rest assured, position never dictates influence. Leadership is not a position. Leadership is serving in a way that influences others to serve. Are you a leader? Do you serve? Do you champion your team? True leaders create a following without ever intending to! Who will you choose to lead, to serve, in your organization today?

♦

Today ___/___/20__ I Will Serve

My God

_____

_____

My Family

_____

_____

My Friends

_____

_____

My Neighbors

_____

_____

A Stranger

_____

_____

"For what we proclaim is not ourselves, but Jesus Christ as Lord, with ourselves as your servants for Jesus' sake."

2 Corinthians 4:5

Join the movement! #Grateful2Serve

◆

Maybe you're not a believer. Maybe you don't understand the benefits of serving God. That's okay. If you've ever been served in any way, no matter how small, you certainly recognize the benefits and joy of being served. Perhaps someone brought you a meal in a time of need. Now, imagine who you can gift that same feeling to today.

◆

Today ___/___/20__ I Will Serve

My God

_____

_____

My Family

_____

_____

My Friends

_____

_____

My Neighbors

_____

_____

A Stranger

_____

_____

"It is the Lord your God you must follow, and him you must revere. Keep his commands and obey him; serve him and hold fast to him."

Deuteronomy 13:14

Join the movement! #Grateful2Serve

♦

You have a direct calling: To serve others. Do you still not know your gifts? An effortless way to find out how you can serve is to ask your loved ones what you're good at. It's sometimes difficult to see the good we have to offer others. Who will you ask today? And how will you use what you hear to serve?

♦

Today ____/____/20____ I Will Serve

My God

_____

_____

My Family

_____

_____

My Friends

_____

_____

My Neighbors

_____

_____

A Stranger

_____

_____

"But if serving the Lord seems undesirable to you, then choose for yourselves this day whom you will serve, whether the gods your ancestors served beyond the Euphrates, or the gods of the Amorites, in whose land you are living. But as for me and my household, we will serve the Lord."

Joshua 24:15

Join the movement! #Grateful2Serve

♦

We serve the Lord God Almighty. We want to honor Him in all we say and do. We pray the same for you and your household.

♦

Join the movement! #Grateful2Serve

Today ___/___/20__ *I Will Serve*

My God

_____

_____

My Family

_____

_____

My Friends

_____

_____

My Neighbors

_____

_____

A Stranger

_____

_____

"And now, Israel, what does the Lord your God ask of you but to fear the Lord your God, to walk in obedience to him, to love him, to serve the Lord your God with all your heart and with all your soul, and to observe the Lord's commands and decrees that I am giving you today for your own good?"

Deuteronomy 10:12-13

Join the movement! #Grateful2Serve

♦

Let's face it, sometimes it just feels good to be selfish as much as we hate to admit it. The problem with that good feeling is that it lasts only a moment. Living a life of serving gives us true lasting joy. We were designed to serve others. To give of our gifts, our talents, and to develop relationships that serve one another. Why? We are incapable of meeting our own needs. If we could meet our own needs, we would have no need for relationships. We need others to serve us. They need us to serve them too. What relationship will you spend time nurturing through service today?

♦

Today ___/___/20__ I Will Serve

My God

_____

_____

My Family

_____

_____

My Friends

_____

_____

My Neighbors

_____

_____

A Stranger

_____

_____

"The Lord will rescue his servants;
no one who takes refuge in him will be condemned."

Psalm 34:22

Join the movement! #Grateful2Serve

♦

Your generosity and service to others will never go unnoticed or unrewarded. It may not be recognized in the way you believe or desire it to be. Be assured, however, that your efforts of service will always grant you many happy returns in ways you may never expect and that often exceed your expectations. How can you serve by exceeding someone's expectations today?

♦

Today ___/___/20__ I Will Serve

My God

_____

_____

My Family

_____

_____

My Friends

_____

_____

My Neighbors

_____

_____

A Stranger

_____

_____

"Serve the Lord with gladness: come before his presence with singing."

Psalm 100:2

Join the movement! #Grateful2Serve

◆

I recall one morning when I went out to get donuts and juice for my house-guests. When I returned home, empty-handed and filled with laughter I was asked where the goods were! I chuckled as I shared the story of a homeless man who was standing by the highway exit. I looked at him, looked at the donuts and juice, and offered him a breakfast of champs! I still smile thinking of this story. Serving and giving brings lasting joy.

◆

Join the movement! #Grateful2Serve

Today ___/___/20__ *I Will Serve*

My God

_____

_____

My Family

_____

_____

My Friends

_____

_____

My Neighbors

_____

_____

A Stranger

_____

_____

*"Then you shall again discern
Between the righteous and the wicked,
Between one who serves God
And one who does not serve Him."*

Malachi 3:18

Join the movement! #Grateful2Serve

◆

Take stock of your intentions today. Do you intend to meet the needs of your family, friends, and coworkers? Or are you looking to find what today has in store for you? You're the best judge of your own intentions. If your intentions are to be a "go getter" today, we challenge you to change your intent a be a go giver!

◆

Today ___/___/20__ *I Will Serve*

My God

_____

_____

My Family

_____

_____

My Friends

_____

_____

My Neighbors

_____

_____

A Stranger

_____

_____

"And do not forget to do good and to share with others, for with such sacrifices God is pleased."

Hebrews 13:16

Join the movement! #Grateful2Serve

♦

Serving really is a sacrifice. Especially when it's a mundane task like taking out the overflowing garbage that nobody else in the house seems to notice! Empty it with gladness and thankfulness for two hands with which to serve.

♦

Today ___/___/20__ I Will Serve

My God

_____

_____

My Family

_____

_____

My Friends

_____

_____

My Neighbors

_____

_____

A stranger

_____

_____

"But when you give to the needy, do not let your left hand know what your right hand is doing, so that your giving may be in secret. And your Father who sees in secret will reward you."

Matthew 6:3

Join the movement! #Grateful2Serve

♦

Your challenge today is to find an opportunity to serve someone in a distinct way...without them knowing! Observe the delight on their faces and don't take credit!

♦

Join the movement! #Grateful2Serve

Today ___/___/20__ I Will Serve

My God

_____

_____

My Family

_____

_____

My Friends

_____

_____

My Neighbors

_____

_____

A stranger

_____

_____

"For if the readiness is there, it is acceptable according to what a person has, not according to what he does not have."

2 Corinthians 8:12

Join the movement! #Grateful2Serve

Thank you for allowing us to serve you! We would be honored to hear how living a life of service for 60 days has changed your life, what you've accomplished, how you've impacted the lives of others, what movements you've created, and what blessings you've given and received!

Share your stories of service with us via email at

Crystel@CrystelandSherri.com

or

Sherri@CrystelandSherri.com

or

#Grateful2Serve to join the movement!

With unconditional gratitude and service,

Sherri and Crystel

Join the movement! #Grateful2Serve

NOTES

Join the movement! #Grateful2Serve

NOTES

Join the movement! #Grateful2Serve

NOTES

Join the movement! #Grateful2Serve

NOTES

Join the movement! #Grateful2Serve

NOTES

Join the movement! #Grateful2Serve

NOTES

Join the movement! #Grateful2Serve

Made in the USA
Middletown, DE
11 November 2021